Citizenship Test

WRITING WORKBOOK

English Version

Fast and Easy way to prepare for the <u>writing</u> section of the citizenship test!

Angelo Tropea

ISBN: 9798665744445

"Success is dependent on effort."

- Sophocles (famous Greek philosopher)

Cover image: Fotolia

Contents

<table>
<tr><td><h1 align="center">Three Parts of the
Citizenship Test</h1></td><td><h1>1</h1></td></tr>
</table>

The writing part of the United States Citizenship Test is one of 3 parts you must pass to become a US citizen.

Part 1. Civics (History, Government and Geography)

At the citizenship interview you will be asked up to 10 questions from the official 100 questions that the government has provided.

To pass this part of the test, you must answer correctly at least 6 of the questions.

The other two parts of the test involve showing some basic ability in English reading and writing. In this book, we will cover the WRITING TEST.

Part 2. English reading

You will be asked to read three (3) sentences containing specific words (less than 100) that the government has announced.

To pass this reading section, you must read one sentence out of the three sentences in a manner suggesting to the USCIS Officer that you appear to understand the meaning of the sentence.

The third part of the test is the <u>WRITING PART</u>.

This is the part that we will practice with this workbook.

Part 3. <u>ENGLISH WRITING</u>

During the citizenship interview, you will be asked to write three (3) sentences containing specific words that the government has published.

There are less than 100 words.

All the <u>writing</u> words are listed in this book.

To pass the writing section, you must write one sentence out of the three sentences in a way that is understandable to the USCIS Officer.

<table>
<tr><td><h1>Overcoming Test Nervousness</h1></td><td><h1>2</h1></td></tr>
</table>

FIRST, TRY <u>NOT</u> TO BE NERVOUS!

If English is not your native language, the writing test may seem hard. <u>This is especially true if your native language uses an alphabet with different characters than the English language</u>.

DON'T WORRY.
THIS BOOK HAS BEEN PREPARED
ESPECIALLY FOR YOU!

Also, if you do feel anxious about taking the writing part of the naturalization test, you should take some comfort in knowing that you are not alone in experiencing such feelings.

Many people, including myself, who have successfully taken many different exams still feel anxious before the next exam. Questions such as "Did I practice enough?" or "Is something suddenly going to happen that will make me fail?" or "Am I going to be so nervous that my mind will go blank?" - and perhaps most terrifying of all, "What is everyone going to say if I fail?"

Like all people, when we feel stress, the body's "fight or flight" response kicks in. We feel threatened and we must decide quickly whether we are going to "run away in fear" or stand our ground and do our best to come out of the situation as a winner.

We can improve our situation greatly - and reduce our anxiety by preparing as much as we can before the test. For example, for the writing questions part of the test, we should prepare with this book and not be afraid to ask for help from a friend or relative. We should replace negative thoughts with thoughts of success and with daily practice.

Although the writing section may seem hard for someone who was not born in the U.S., the words are few - and very easy to study. In this book we will break down the large chunks of the WRITING WORDS information into small pieces so that it will be easy for you to practice and remember them.

<table>
<tr><td><h1 style="text-align:center">OFFICIAL LIST
OF WRITING WORDS</h1></td><td>3</td></tr>
</table>

FIRST, let's take a brief look at the writing words that we must know how to write:

WRITING WORDS

PEOPLE (3 last names of famous American Presidents)
Adams Lincoln Washington

CIVICS (words that have to do with the rights and duties of citizenship, and American history)	
American Indians	free
capital	freedom of speech
citizens	President
Civil War	Right
Congress	Senators
Father of Our Country	State / States
flag	White House

PLACES	
(American states and cities)	
Alaska	New York City
California	United States
Canada	Washington (a state, or
Delaware	President Washington)
Mexico	Washington, D.C. (city)

MONTHS	
(7 of the 12 months of the year)	
February	September
May	October
June	November
July	

VERBS	
(words that have to do with some action or state of being)	
can	lives / lived
come	meets
elect	pay
have / has	vote
is / was / be	want

HOLIDAYS	
(7 United States holidays)	
Presidents' Day	Labor Day
Memorial Day	Columbus Day
Flag Day	Thanksgiving
Independence Day	

<table>
<tr><td colspan="2" align="center"><u>OTHER WORDS</u>
(25 easy words)</td></tr>
<tr><td align="center">and
during
for
here
in
of
on
the
to
we
blue
dollar bill
fifty / 50</td><td align="center">first
largest
most
north
one
one hundred / 100
people
red
second
south
taxes
white</td></tr>
</table>

<table>
<tr><td>

How to practice
WRITING THE OFFICIAL WORDS

</td><td>

4

</td></tr>
</table>

First, look at the official words listed in pages 8-10. If English is not your native language or your native language uses different symbols, practice writing the words until you become comfortable writing them. Examples of how to write all the words (hand printed or in the form of script (longhand) are included for every word).

<u>HOW TO PRACTICE</u>

1. Have a friend or relative read the official words to you.

2. On a piece of paper, write the words, either in printed letters or in long hand (script).

3. Check to see if you wrote the words correctly.

<u>HOW TO USE THE PRACTICE SENTENCES</u>

1. Have a friend or relative read each sentence to you.

2. On a piece of paper, write the sentence, either in printed letters or in long hand (script).

3. Check to see if you spelled each word correctly.

The more you practice, the easier it will become and the better you will do!

NOTE: IF A FRIEND OR RELATIVE IS NOT AVAILBLE TO READ THE WORDS, WE HAVE A VIDEO ON YOUTUBE THAT WILL READ THE WORDS AND SENTENCES TO YOU SO THAT YOU CAN PRACTIVE THEM.

THIS VIDEO IS AT:

https://www.youtube.com/watch?v=P7lFvKYUbM4

This video has been seen more than 238,000 times!

The lessons in this book are the same as in the YouTube video.

Good Luck!

Let's Practice Writing Words and Sentences	**5**

During the naturalization interview, you will be expected to write correctly at least one of the three sentences that will be spoken by the interviewer. Each sentence will contain some of the 82 words and phrases that are on the official list of words you must know.

In this book we will practice writing the words and then writing sentences that are made up only of words that are on the official list.

The first three words on the list are the last names of three Americans:

They are: 1. Adams,

                2. Lincoln,

                3. Washington.

Each of them was President of the United States.

The following three sentences (which we will practice after we practice the words) are all made up of the three names and 7 other words that are on the official list:

   1. Adams was the second President of the United States.

   2. Lincoln was President during the Civil War.

   3. Washington was the first President of the United

      States.

The 10 official words that make up the 3 sentences are:

1. Adams
2. Lincoln
3. Washington
4. Civil War
5. President

6. United States
7. was
8. during
9. of
10. the

We will first practice writing each word, and then we will practice writing the 3 sentences.

Ready?

<u>Adams</u>

The first word is **<u>Adams</u>**. Please look at the word and try to memorize the spelling: **A d a m s.**

On a piece of paper, please write the word **<u>Adams</u>.**

(An example of the correct spelling of <u>Adams</u> - in printed form, handwritten form, and script (long-hand form) is on the following page.

<u>Adams</u>

<u>Adams</u>

<u>Adams</u>

This is the correct spelling of Adams - in printed form, handwritten form, and script (long-hand form).

<u>Lincoln</u>

The next word is **<u>Lincoln</u>**. Please look at the word and try to memorize the spelling: **<u>L i n c o l n</u>.**

On a piece of paper, please write the word **<u>Lincoln</u>**.

An example of the correct spelling of <u>Lincoln</u> - in printed form, handwritten form, and script (long-hand form) is on the following page.

Lincoln

Lincoln

Lincoln

This is the correct spelling of <u>Lincoln</u> - in printed form, handwritten form, and script (long-hand form).

<u>Washington</u>

The next word is **<u>Washington</u>**. Please look at the word and try to memorize the spelling: **<u>W a s h i n g t o n</u>.**

On a piece of paper, please write the word **<u>Washington</u>**.

An example of the correct spelling of <u>Washington</u> - in printed form, handwritten form, and script (long-hand form) is on the following page.

<u>Washington</u>

Washington

Washington

This is the correct spelling of <u>Washington</u> in printed form, handwritten form, and script (long-hand form).

<u>Civil War</u>

The next words are **<u>Civil War</u>**. Please look at the words and try to memorize the spelling: **<u>C i v i l W a r</u>.**

On a piece of paper, please write the words **<u>Civil War</u>**.

<u>President</u>

The next word is **<u>President</u>**. Please look at the words and try to memorize the spelling: **<u>P r e s i d e n t</u>.**

On a piece of paper, please write the word **<u>President</u>**.

<u>United States</u>

The next words are **<u>United States</u>**. Please look at the words and try to memorize the spelling: **<u>U n i t e d S t a t e s</u>.**

On a piece of paper, please write the words **<u>United States</u>**.

<u>was</u>

The next word is **<u>was</u>**. Please look at the word and try to memorize the spelling: **<u>w a s</u>.**

On a piece of paper, please write the word **<u>was</u>**.

Example of the correct spelling of the above words in printed form, handwritten form, and script (long-hand form) are on the following page.

Civil War

Civil War

Civil War

President

President

President

United States

United States

United States

was

was

was

during

The next word is **during**. Please look at the words and try to memorize the spelling: **d u r i n g.**

On a piece of paper, please write the word **during**.

of

The next word is **of**. Please look at the word and try to memorize the spelling: **o f.**

On a piece of paper, please write the word **of**.

the

The next word is **the**. Please look at the word and try to memorize the spelling: **t h e.**

On a piece of paper, please write the word **the**.

Now let's practice writing three sentences that are made up of the 10 words we have just reviewed.

The first sentence is the following:

Adams was the second President of the United States.

Please look at the above sentence and try to memorize the spelling of the sentence:
On a piece of paper, please write the sentence.

(Examples of the correct spelling of the above words and sentence in printed form, handwritten form, and script (long-hand form) are on the following page.)

<u>during</u>

during

during

<u>of</u>

of

of

<u>the</u>

the

the

<u>Adams was the second President of the United States.</u>

Adams was the second President of the United States.

Adams was the second President of the United States.

<u>Lincoln was President during the Civil War.</u>

Please look at the above sentence and try to memorize the spelling of the sentence.
On a piece of paper, please write the sentence.

<u>Washington was the first President of the United States.</u>

Please look at the above sentence and try to memorize the spelling of the sentence.
On a piece of paper, please write the sentence.

The next 10 words are:	
1. Congress	6. can
2. is	7. vote
3. in	8. people
4. Washington, D.C.	9. have
5. American Indians	10. freedom of speech

<u>Congress</u>

The next word is **Congress**. Please look at the word and try to memorize the spelling: **C o n g r e s s.**

On a piece of paper, please write the word **Congress**.

<u>is</u>

The next word is **is**. Please look at the word and try to memorize the spelling: **i s.**

On a piece of paper, please write the word **is**.

Examples of the correct spelling of the above words and sentence in printed form, handwritten form, and script (long-hand form) are on the following page.

Lincoln was President during the Civil War.

Lincoln was President during the Civil War.

Lincoln was President during the Civil War.

Washington was the first President of the United States.

Washington was the first President of the United States.

Washington was the first President of the United States.

Congress

Congress

Congress

is

is

is

<u>in</u>

The next word is <u>**in**</u>. Please look at the word and try to memorize the spelling: <u>**i n.**</u>

On a piece of paper, please write the word <u>**in**</u>.

<u>Washington, D.C.</u>

The next words are <u>**Washington, D.C.**</u> Please look at the words and try to memorize the spelling: <u>**W a s h i n g t o n, D.C.**</u>

On a piece of paper, please write the words <u>**Washington D.C.**</u>

<u>American Indians</u>

The next words are <u>**American Indians.**</u> Please look at the words and try to memorize the spelling: <u>**A m e r i c a n I n d i a n s.**</u>

On a piece of paper, please write the words <u>**American Indians**</u>

<u>can</u>

The next word is <u>**can**</u>. Please look at the word and try to memorize the spelling: <u>**c a n.**</u>

On a piece of paper, please write the word <u>**can**</u>.

Examples of the correct spelling of the above words in printed form, handwritten form, and script (long-hand form) are on the following page.)

<u>in</u>   <u>Washington, D. C.</u>

_______in_______   _Washington, D.C._

_______in_______   _Washington, D.C._

<u>American Indians</u>   <u>can</u>

American Indians   ___can___

American Indians   ___can___

<u>vote</u>

The next word is <u>**vote**</u>. Please look at the word and try to memorize the spelling: <u>**v o t e.**</u>

On a piece of paper, please write the word <u>**vote**</u>.

<u>people</u>

The next word is <u>**people**</u>. Please look at the word and try to memorize the spelling: <u>**p e o p l e.**</u>

On a piece of paper, please write the word <u>**people**</u>.

<u>have</u>

The next word is <u>**have**</u>. Please look at the word and try to memorize the spelling: <u>**h a v e.**</u>

On a piece of paper, please write the word <u>**have**</u>.

<u>freedom of speech</u>

The next words are <u>**freedom of speech**</u>. Please look at the words and try to memorize the spelling: <u>**f r e e d o m o f s p c c c h.**</u>

On a piece of paper, please write the words <u>**freedom of speech**</u>.

Examples of the correct spelling of the above words in printed form, handwritten form, and script (long-hand form) are on the following page.

<u>vote</u>

<u>people</u>

vote

people

vote

people

<u>have</u>

<u>freedom of speech</u>

have

freedom of speech

have

freedom of speech

Now let's practice writing three sentences that are made up of the 10 words we have just reviewed.

The first sentence is the following:

<u>Congress is in Washington, D.C.</u>

Please look at the above sentence and try to memorize the spelling of the sentence.
On a piece of paper, please write the sentence.

<u>American Indians can vote.</u>

Please look at the above sentence and try to memorize the spelling of the sentence.
On a piece of paper, please write the sentence.

<u>People have freedom of speech.</u>

Please look at the above sentence and try to memorize the spelling of the sentence.
On a piece of paper, please write the sentence.

The next 11 official words are:	
1. Canada	6. citizens
2. North	7. want
3. has	8. to
4. one hundred / 100	9. and
5. Senators	10. Presidents' Day
	11. February

<u>Canada</u>

The next word is **<u>Canada</u>**. Please look at the word and try to memorize the spelling: **<u>C a n a d a</u>**.

On a piece of paper, please write the word **<u>Canada</u>**.

<u>Congress is in
Washington, D.C.</u>

Congress is in
Washington, D.C.

Congress is in
Washington, D.C.

<u>American Indians can vote.</u>

American Indians can vote.

American Indians can vote.
American Indians can vote.

<u>People have freedom
of speech.</u>

People have freedom
of speech.

People have freedom
of speech.

<u>Canada</u>

Canada

Canada

<u>north</u>

The next word is **<u>north</u>**. Please look at the word and try to memorize the spelling: **<u>n o r t h.</u>**

On a piece of paper, please write the word **<u>north</u>**.

<u>has</u>

The next word is **<u>has</u>**. Please look at the word and try to memorize the spelling: **<u>h a s.</u>**

On a piece of paper, please write the word **<u>has</u>**.

<u>one hundred / 100</u>

The next words are **<u>one hundred / 100</u>**. Please look at the words and try to memorize the spelling: **<u>o n e h u n d r e d / 100.</u>**

On a piece of paper, please write the words **<u>one hundred / 100</u>**.

<u>Senators</u>

The next word is **<u>Senators</u>**. Please look at the word and try to memorize the spelling: **<u>S e n a t o r s.</u>**

On a piece of paper, please write the word **<u>Senators</u>**.

Examples of the correct spelling of the above words in printed form, handwritten form, and script (long-hand form) are on the following page.

<u>north</u>

north

north

<u>has</u>

has

has

<u>one hundred/100</u>

one hundred/100

one hundred/100

<u>Senators</u>

Senators

Senators

<u>citizens</u>

The next word is **<u>citizens</u>**. Please look at the word and try to memorize the spelling: **<u>c i t i z e n s</u>.**

On a piece of paper, please write the word **<u>citizens</u>**.

<u>want</u>

The next word is **<u>want</u>**. Please look at the word and try to memorize the spelling: **<u>w a n t</u>.**

On a piece of paper, please write the word **<u>want</u>**.

<u>to</u>

The next word is **<u>to</u>**. Please look at the word and try to memorize the spelling: **<u>t o</u>.**

On a piece of paper, please write the word **<u>to</u>**.

<u>and</u>

The next word is **<u>and</u>**. Please look at the word and try to memorize the spelling: **<u>a n d</u>.**

On a piece of paper, please write the word **<u>and</u>**.

<u>citizens</u>

citizens

citizens

<u>want</u>

want

want

<u>to</u>

to

to

<u>and</u>

and

and

February

The next word is **February**. Please look at the word and try to memorize the spelling: **F e b r u a r y**.

On a piece of paper, please write the word **February**.

Now let's practice writing three sentences that are made up of the 10 words we have just reviewed.

The first sentence is the following:

Canada is in the north.

The next sentence is **Canada is in the north**. Please look at the words and try to memorize the spelling: **C a n a da i s i n t h e n o r t h**.

On a piece of paper, please write the sentence **Canada is in the north**.

Congress has one hundred / 100 Senators

The next sentence is **Congress has one hundred / 100 Senators**.

Please look at the words and try to memorize the spelling: **C o n g r e s s h a s o n e h u n d r e d / 100 S e n a t o r s**.

On a piece of paper, please write the sentence **Congress has one hundred / 100 Senators**.

Citizens want to vote and be free.

The next sentence is **Citizens want to vote and be free**. Please look at the words and try to memorize the spelling: **C i t i z e n s w a n t to v o t e a n d b e f r e e**.

On a piece of paper, please write the sentence **Citizens want to vote and be free**.

February

February

February

Canada is in the north.

Canada is in the north.

Canada is in the north.

Congress has one hundred/100 Senators.

Congress has one hundred/100 Senators.

Congress has one hundred/100 Senators.

Citizens want to vote and be free.

Citizens want to vote and be free.

Citizens want to vote and be free.

Presidents' Day is in February.

The next sentence is **Presidents' Day is in February.** Please look at the words and try to memorize the spelling: **P r e s i d e n t s' D a y is in F e b r u a r y.**

On a piece of paper, please write the sentence **Presidents' Day is in February.**

The next 10 official words are:	
1. Father of Our Country	6. Flag Day
2. Memorial Day	7. June
3. May	8. White House
4. Independence Day	9. fifty/ 50
5. July	10. states

Father of Our Country

The next words are **Father of Our Country.** Please look at the words and try to memorize the spelling: **F a t h e r o f O u r C o u n t r y.**

On a piece of paper, please write the words **Father of Our Country**

Memorial Day

The next words are **Memorial Day.** Please look at the words and try to memorize the spelling: **M e m o r i a l D a y.**

On a piece of paper, please write the words **Memorial Day.**

May

The next word is **May.** Please look at the word and try to memorize the spelling: **M a y.**

On a piece of paper, please write the word **May.**

President's Day is in February.

President's Day is in February.

President's Day is in February.

Father of Our Country

Father of Our Country

Father of Our Country

Memorial Day

Memorial Day

Memorial Day

May

May

May

Independence Day

The next words are **Independence Day**. Please look at the words and try to memorize the spelling: **I n d e p e n d e n c e D a y.**

On a piece of paper, please write the words **Independence Day**.

July

The next word is **July**. Please look at the word and try to memorize the spelling: **J u l y.**

On a piece of paper, please write the word **July**.

Flag Day

The next words are **Flag Day**. Please look at the words and try to memorize the spelling: **F l a g D a y.**

On a piece of paper, please write the words **Flag Day**.

June

The next word is **June**. Please look at the word and try to memorize the spelling: **J u n e.**

On a piece of paper, please write the word **June**.

<u>Independence Day</u>

Independence Day

Independence Day

<u>July</u>

July

July

<u>Flag Day</u>

Flag Day

Flag Day

<u>June</u>

June

June

<u>White House</u>

The next words are <u>**White House**</u>. Please look at the words and try to memorize the spelling: <u>**W h i t e   H o u s e.**</u>

On a piece of paper, please write the words <u>**White House**</u>.

<u>fifty / 50</u>

The next word is <u>**fifty / 50**</u>. Please look at the word and try to memorize the spelling: <u>**f i f ty / 50.**</u>

On a piece of paper, please write the word <u>**fifty / 50**</u>.

<u>states</u>

The next word is <u>**states**</u>. Please look at the word and try to memorize the spelling: <u>**s t a t e s.**</u>

On a piece of paper, please write the word <u>**states**</u>.

Now let's practice writing three sentences that are made up of the 10 words we have just reviewed.

The first sentence is the following:

<u>Washington is the Father of Our Country.</u>

The next sentence is <u>**Washington is the Father of Our Country**</u>. Please look at the words and try to memorize the spelling: <u>**W a s h i n g t o n   i s   t h e   F a t h e r   o f   O u r   C o u n t r y.**</u>

On a piece of paper, please write the sentence <u>**Washington is the Father of Our Country**</u>.

<u>White House</u>

White House

White House

<u>fifty/50</u>

fifty/50

fifty/50

<u>states</u>

states

states

<u>Washington is the
Father of Our Country.</u>

_Washington is the
Father of Our Country_

_Washington is the
Father of Our Country._

<u>Memorial Day is in May</u>.

The next sentence is <u>**Memorial Day is in May**</u>. Please look at the words and try to memorize the spelling: <u>**M e m o r i a l   D a y   i s   i n   M a y**</u>.

On a piece of paper, please write the sentence <u>**Memorial Day is in May**</u>.

<u>Independence Day is in July</u>.

The next sentence is <u>**Independence Day is in July**</u>. Please look at the words and try to memorize the spelling: <u>**I n d e p e n d e n c e   D a y   i s   i n   J u l y**</u>.

On a piece of paper, please write the sentence <u>**Independence Day is in July**</u>.

<u>Flag Day is in June</u>.

The next sentence is <u>**Flag Day is in June**</u>. Please look at the words and try to memorize the spelling: <u>**F l a g   D a y   i s   i n J u n e**</u>.

On a piece of paper, please write the sentence <u>**Flag Day is in June**</u>.

<u>The White House is in Washington, D.C.</u>

The next sentence is <u>**The White House is in Washington, D.C.**</u> Please look at the words and try to memorize the spelling: <u>**T h e   W h i t e   H o u s e   i s   i n   W a s h i n g t o n, D. C.**</u>

On a piece of paper, please write the sentence <u>**The White House is in Washington, D.C.**</u>

<u>Memorial Day is in May.</u>

<u>Memorial Day is in May.</u>

<u>Memorial Day is in May.</u>

<u>Independence Day is in July.</u>

<u>Independence Day is in July.</u>

<u>Independence Day is in July.</u>

<u>Flag Day is in June.</u>

<u>Flag Day is in June.</u>

<u>Flag Day is in June.</u>

<u>The White House is in
Washington, D.C.</u>

<u>The White House is in
Washington D.C.</u>

<u>The White House is in
Washington, D.C.</u>

The United States has fifty / 50 states.

The next sentence is **The United States has fifty / 50 states.** Please look at the words and try to memorize the spelling:
The United States has fifty/50 states.

On a piece of paper, please write the sentence: **The United States has fifty / 50 states.**

The next 10 official words are:	
1. Labor Day	6. New York City
2. September	7. flag
3. Alaska	8. red
4. California	9. white
5. Delaware	10. blue

Labor Day

The next words are **Labor Day**. Please look at the words and try to memorize the spelling: **L a b o r D a y.**

On a piece of paper, please write the words **Labor Day**.

September

The next word is **September**. Please look at the word and try to memorize the spelling: **S e p t e m b e r.**

On a piece of paper, please write the word **September**.

Alaska

The next word is **Alaska**. Please look at the word and try to memorize the spelling: **A l a s k a.**

On a piece of paper, please write the word **Alaska**.

The United States has
fifty/50 states.

The United States has
fifty/50 states.

The United States has
fifty/50 states.

Labor Day

Labor Day

Labor Day

September

September

September

Alaska

Alaska

Alaska

California

The next word is **California**. Please look at the word and try to memorize the spelling: **C a l i f o r n i a.**

On a piece of paper, please write the word **California**.

Delaware

The next word is **Delaware**. Please look at the word and try to memorize the spelling: **D e l a w a r e.**

On a piece of paper, please write the word **Delaware**.

New York City

The next words are **New York City**. Please look at the words and try to memorize the spelling: **N e w   Y o r k   C i t y.**

On a piece of paper, please write the words **New York City**.

flag

The next word is **flag**. Please look at the word and try to memorize the spelling: **f l a g.**

On a piece of paper, please write the word **flag**.

<u>California</u>

California

California

<u>Delaware</u>

Delaware

Delaware

<u>New York City</u>

New York City

New York City

<u>flag</u>

flag

flag

<u>red</u>

The next word is **<u>red</u>**. Please look at the word and try to memorize the spelling: **<u>r e d</u>.**

On a piece of paper, please write the word **<u>red</u>**.

<u>white</u>

The next word is **<u>white</u>**. Please look at the word and try to memorize the spelling: **<u>w h i t e</u>.**

On a piece of paper, please write the word **<u>white</u>**.

<u>blue</u>

The next word is **<u>blue</u>**. Please look at the word and try to memorize the spelling: **<u>blue</u>.**

On a piece of paper, please write the word **<u>blue</u>**.

Now let's practice writing four sentences that are made up of the 10 words we have just reviewed.

The first sentence is the following:

<u>Labor Day is in September.</u>

The next sentence is **<u>Labor Day is in September</u>**. Please look at the words and try to memorize the spelling: **<u>L a b o r D a y i s i n S e p t e m b e r</u>.**

On a piece of paper, please write the sentence **<u>Labor Day is in September</u>**.

<u>red</u>

red

red

<u>white</u>

white

white

<u>blue</u>

blue

blue

<u>Labor Day is in September.</u>

Labor Day is in September.

Labor Day is in September.

Alaska is north of California.

The next sentence is **Alaska is north of California.** Please look at the words and try to memorize the spelling: **A l a s k a i s n o r t h of C a l i f o r n i a.**

On a piece of paper, please write the sentence **Alaska is north of California.**

Delaware is South of New York City.

The next sentence is **Delaware is south of New York City.** Please look at the words and try to memorize the spelling: **D e l a w a r e i s s o u t h o f N e w Y o r k C i t y.**

On a piece of paper, please write the sentence **Delaware is south of New York City.**

The flag is red, white and blue.

The next sentence is **The flag is red, white and blue.** Please look at the words and try to memorize the spelling: **T h e f l a g i s r e d, w h i t e a n d b l u e.**

On a piece of paper, please write the sentence **The flag is red, white and blue.**

The next 10 official words are:	
1. lives	6. Columbus Day
2. lived	7. October
3. we	8. on
4. pay	9. one
5. taxes	10.dollar bill

Alaska is north of California.

Delaware is south of
New York City.

The flag is red, white,
and blue.

<u>lives</u>

The next word is **<u>lives</u>**. Please look at the word and try to memorize the spelling: **<u>l i v e s.</u>**

On a piece of paper, please write the word **<u>lives</u>**.

<u>lived</u>

The next word is **<u>lived</u>**. Please look at the word and try to memorize the spelling: **<u>l i v e d.</u>**

On a piece of paper, please write the word **<u>lived</u>**.

<u>we</u>

The next word is **<u>we</u>**. Please look at the word and try to memorize the spelling: **<u>w e.</u>**

On a piece of paper, please write the word **<u>we</u>**.

<u>pay</u>

The next word is **<u>pay</u>**. Please look at the word and try to memorize the spelling: **<u>p a y.</u>**

On a piece of paper, please write the word **<u>pay</u>**.

<u>lives</u>

lives

lives

<u>lived</u>

lived

lived

<u>we</u>

we

we

<u>pay</u>

pay

pay

<u>taxes</u>

The next word is **<u>taxes</u>**. Please look at the word and try to memorize the spelling: **<u>t a x e s</u>.**

On a piece of paper, please write the word **<u>taxes</u>**.

<u>Columbus Day</u>

The next words are **<u>Columbus Day</u>**. Please look at the words and try to memorize the spelling: **<u>C o l u m b u s D a y</u>.**

On a piece of paper, please write the words **<u>Columbus Day</u>**.

<u>October</u>

The next word is **<u>October</u>**. Please look at the word and try to memorize the spelling: **<u>O c t o b e r</u>.**

On a piece of paper, please write the word **<u>October</u>**.

<u>on</u>

The next word is **<u>on</u>**. Please look at the word and try to memorize the spelling: **<u>o n</u>.**

On a piece of paper, please write the word **<u>on</u>**.

<u>taxes</u>

taxes

taxes

<u>Columbus Day</u>

Columbus Day

Columbus Day

<u>October</u>

October

October

<u>on</u>

on

on

<u>one</u>

The next word is **<u>one</u>**. Please look at the word and try to memorize the spelling: **<u>o n e</u>.**

On a piece of paper, please write the word **<u>one</u>**.

<u>dollar bill</u>

The next words are **<u>dollar bill</u>**. Please look at the words and try to memorize the spelling: **<u>d o l l a r b i l l</u>.**

On a piece of paper, please write the words **<u>dollar bill</u>**.

Now let's practice writing five sentences that are made up of the 10 words we have just reviewed.

<u>The President lives in the White House</u>.

The first sentence is **<u>The President lives in the White House.</u>** Please look at the words and try to memorize the spelling:
<u>T h e P r e s i d e n t l i v e s i n t h e W h i t e H o u s e</u>.

On a piece of paper, please write the sentence
<u>The President lives in the White House</u>.

<u>Washington lived in Washington, D.C.</u>

The next sentence is **<u>Washington lived in Washington D.C</u>.**
Please look at the words and try to memorize the spelling:
<u>W a s h i n g t o n l i v e d i n W a s h i n g t o n D. C.</u>

On a piece of paper, please write the sentence
<u>Washington lived in Washington D.C</u>.

<u>one</u>

one

one

<u>dollar bill</u>

dollar bill

dollar bill

<u>The President lives in
the White House.</u>

The President lives in
the White House.

*The President lives in
the White House.*

<u>Washington lived in
Washington, D.C.</u>

Washington lived in
Washington, D.C.

*Washington lived in
Washington, D.C.*

<u>We pay taxes.</u>

The next sentence is **<u>We pay taxes.</u>**
Please look at the words and try to memorize the spelling:
<u>We pay taxe s</u>.

On a piece of paper, please write the sentence **<u>We pay taxes.</u>**

<u>Columbus Day is in October.</u>

The next sentence is **<u>Columbus Day is in October.</u>**
Please look at the words and try to memorize the spelling:
<u>Columbus Day is in October</u>.

On a piece of paper, please write the sentence
<u>Columbus Day is in October</u>.

<u>Washington is on the one dollar bill.</u>

The next sentence is **<u>Washington is on the one dollar bill.</u>**
Please look at the words and try to memorize the spelling:
<u>Washington is on the one dollar bill</u>.

On a piece of paper, please write the sentence:
<u>Washington is on the one dollar bill</u>.

<u>The next 13 official writing words are:</u>	
1. largest	8. most
2. Thanksgiving	9. Mexico
3. November	10. here
4. meets	11. for
5. elect	12. and
6. capital	13. come
7. right	

We pay taxes.

Columbus Day is in October.

We pay taxes

Columbus Day is in October.

We pay taxes.

Columbus Day is in October.

Washington is on the one
dollar bill.

Washington is on the one
dollar bill.

Washington is on the one
dollar bill.

largest

The next word is **largest**.
Please look at the words and try to memorize the spelling: **l a r g e s t**.

On a piece of paper, please write the word **largest**.

Thanksgiving

The next word is **Thanksgiving**.
Please look at the word and try to memorize the spelling:
T h a n k s g i v i n g.

On a piece of paper, please write the word **Thanksgiving**.

November

The next word is **November**.
Please look at the word and try to memorize the spelling:
N o v e m b e r.

On a piece of paper, please write the word **November**.

meets

The next word is **meets**.
Please look at the word and try to memorize the spelling: **m e e t s**.

On a piece of paper, please write the word **meets**.

largest

largest

largest

Thanksgiving

Thanksgiving

Thanksgiving

November

November

November

meets

meets

meets

<u>elect</u>

The next word is **<u>elect</u>**.
Please look at the word and try to memorize the spelling: **<u>e l e c t</u>**.

On a piece of paper, please write the word **<u>elect</u>**.

<u>capital</u>

The next word is **<u>capital</u>**.
Please look at the word and try to memorize the spelling: **<u>c a p i t a l</u>**.

On a piece of paper, please write the word **<u>capital</u>**.

<u>right</u>

The next word is **<u>right</u>**.
Please look at the word and try to memorize the spelling: **<u>r i g h t</u>**.

On a piece of paper, please write the word **<u>right</u>**.

<u>most</u>

The next word is **<u>most</u>**.
Please look at the word and try to memorize the spelling: **<u>m o s t</u>**.

On a piece of paper, please write the word **<u>most</u>**.

elect

elect

elect

capital

capital

capital

right

right

right

most

most

most

<u>Mexico</u>

The next word is **<u>Mexico</u>**.
Please look at the word and try to memorize the spelling: **<u>M e x i c o</u>.**

On a piece of paper, please write the word **<u>Mexico</u>**.

<u>here</u>

The next word is **<u>here</u>**.
Please look at the word and try to memorize the spelling: **<u>h e r e</u>.**

On a piece of paper, please write the word **<u>here</u>**.

<u>for</u>

The next word is **<u>for</u>**.
Please look at the word and try to memorize the spelling: **<u>f o r</u>.**

On a piece of paper, please write the word **<u>for</u>**.

<u>and</u>

The next word is **<u>and</u>**.
Please look at the word and try to memorize the spelling: **<u>a n d</u>.**

On a piece of paper, please write the word **<u>and</u>**.

<u>Mexico</u>

Mexico

Mexico

<u>here</u>

here

here

<u>for</u>

for

for

<u>and</u>

and

and

<u>**come**</u>

The next word is <u>**come**</u>.
Please look at the word and try to memorize the spelling: <u>**c o m e**</u>.

On a piece of paper, please write the word <u>**come**</u>.

Now let's practice writing eleven sentences that are made up of the 13 words we have just reviewed.

<u>**Alaska is the largest state.**</u>

The first sentence is <u>**Alaska is the largest state.**</u>
Please look at the words and try to memorize the spelling:
<u>**A l a s k a   i s   t h e   l a r g e s t   s t a t e.**</u>

On a piece of paper, please write the sentence
<u>**Alaska is the largest state.**</u>

<u>**Thanksgiving is in November.**</u>

The next sentence is <u>**Thanksgiving is in November.**</u>
Please look at the words and try to memorize the spelling:
<u>**T h a n k s g i v i n g   i s   i n   N o v e m b e r.**</u>

On a piece of paper, please write the sentence
<u>**Thanksgiving is in November.**</u>

<u>**Congress meets in Washington, D.C.**</u>

The next sentence is <u>**Congress meets in Washington, D.C.**</u>
Please look at the words and try to memorize the spelling:
<u>**C o n g r e s s   m e e t s   i n   W a s h i n g t o n, D.C.**</u>

On a piece of paper, please write the sentence:
<u>**Congress meets in Washington, D.C.**</u>

<u>come</u>

come

come

<u>Alaska is the largest state.</u>

Alaska is the largest state.

Alaska is the largest state.

<u>Thanksgiving is in November.</u>

Thanksgiving is in November.

Thanksgiving is in November.

<u>Congress meets in Washington, D.C.</u>

Congress meets in Washington, D.C.

Congress meets in Washington, D.C.

<u>Citizens of states elect Senators.</u>

The next sentence is <u>**Citizens of states elect Senators.**</u>
Please look at the words and try to memorize the spelling:
<u>**Citizens of states elect Senators.**</u>

On a piece of paper, please write the sentence
<u>**Citizens of states elect Senators.**</u>

<u>The capital is Washington, D.C.</u>

The next sentence is <u>**The capital is Washington, D.C.**</u>
Please look at the words and try to memorize the spelling:
<u>**The capital is Washington, D.C.**</u>

On a piece of paper, please write the sentence
<u>**The capital is Washington, D.C.**</u>

<u>Freedom of speech is a right.</u>

The next sentence is <u>**Freedom of speech is a right.**</u>
Please look at the words and try to memorize the spelling:
<u>**Freedom of speech is a right.**</u>

On a piece of paper, please write the sentence:
<u>**Freedom of speech is a right.**</u>

<u>Most citizens vote.</u>

The next sentence is <u>**Most citizens vote.**</u>
Please look at the words and try to memorize the spelling:
<u>**Most citizens vote.**</u>

On a piece of paper, please write the sentence:
<u>**Most citizens vote.**</u>

Citizens of states elect Senators.

Citizens of states
elect Senators.

Citizens of states
elect Senators.

The capital is Washington, D.C.

The capital is
Washington, D.C.

The capital is
Washington, D.C.

Freedom of speech is a right.

Freedom of speech
is a right.

Freedom of speech
is a right.

Most citizens vote.

Most citizens vote.

Most citizens vote.

Mexico is south of the United States.

The next sentence is **Mexico is south of the United States.**
Please look at the words and try to memorize the spelling:
Mexico is south of the United States.

On a piece of paper, please write the sentence
Mexico is south of the United States.

American Indians lived here.

The next sentence is **American Indians lived here.**
Please look at the words and try to memorize the spelling:
American Indians lived here.

On a piece of paper, please write the sentence
American Indians lived here.

Citizens vote for Senators and the President.

The next sentence is: **Citizens vote for Senators and the President.**
Please look at the words and try to memorize the spelling:
Citizens vote for Senators and the President.

On a piece of paper, please write the sentence:
Citizens vote for Senators and the President.

Citizens come to vote.

The next sentence is **Citizens come to vote.**
Please look at the words and try to memorize the spelling:
Citizens come to vote.

On a piece of paper, please write the sentence:
Citizens come to vote.

Mexico is south of the
United States.

American Indians lived here.

Citizens vote for Senators and
the President.

Citizens come to vote.

Extra Writing Practice	**6**

1. Have a friend or relative read each sentence to you.

2. On a piece of paper, write the sentence, either in printed letters or in long hand (script).

3. Check to see if you spelled each word correctly.

Sentence Example

1	We pay taxes. (computer printed) We pay taxes. (hand-written print) We pay taxes. (hand-written script - long-hand)

The more you practice, the easier it becomes and the better you will do!

Sentences 1 - 100

1	We pay taxes. We pay taxes. We pay taxes.
2	The flag is here. The flag is here. The flag is here.

3	Citizens can vote. Citizens can vote. Citizens can vote.
4	People can be free. People can be free. People can be free.
5	Alaska is a state. Alaska is a state. Alaska is a state.
6	Pay for the flag. Pay for the flag. Pay for the flag.
7	We want to vote. We want to vote. We want to vote.
8	Citizens pay taxes. Citizens pay taxes. Citizens pay taxes.

9	We lived in Canada. We lived in Canada. We lived in Canada.
10	Pay here for the flag. Pay here for the flag. Pay here for the flag.
11	Most people can vote. Most people can vote. Most people can vote.
12	Flag Day is in June. Flag Day is in June. Flag Day is in June.
13	Pay for the largest flag. Pay for the largest flag. Pay for the largest flag.
14	The largest flag is free. The largest flag is free. The largest flag is free.

15	Senators vote for taxes. Senators vote for taxes. Senators vote for taxes.
16	One state is Delaware. One state is Delaware. One state is Delaware.
17	People want to be free. People want to be free. People want to be free.
18	Adams was President. Adams was President. Adams was President.
19	Washington is one State. Washington is one State. Washington is one State.
20	The Senators vote here. The Senators vote here. The Senators vote here.

21	Citizens elect the Senators. Citizens elect the Senators. Citizens elect the Senators.
22	Alaska is the largest state. Alaska is the largest state. Alaska is the largest state.
23	Alaska is north of Mexico. Alaska is north of Mexico. Alaska is north of Mexico.
24	Mexico is south of Canada. Mexico is south of Canada. Mexico is south of Canada.
25	Memorial Day is in May. Memorial Day is in May. Memorial Day is in May.
26	Independence Day is in July. Independence Day is in July. Independence Day is in July.

27	Labor Day is in September. Labor Day is in September. Labor Day is in September.
28	Columbus Day is in October. Columbus Day is in October. Columbus Day is in October.
29	The Senators want to vote. The Senators want to vote. The Senators want to vote.
30	The White House is white. The White House is white. The White House is white.
31	Delaware is north of Mexico. Delaware is north of Mexico. Delaware is north of Mexico.
32	Citizens vote in November. Citizens vote in November. Citizens vote in November.

33	Come to the White House. Come to the White House. Come to the White House.
34	Is Canada the largest state? Is Canada the largest state? Is Canada the largest state? (Canada is a country.)
35	American Indians can vote. American Indians can vote. American Indians can vote.
36	One Right is the right to vote. One Right is the right to vote. One Right is the right to vote.
37	The largest state is Alaska. The largest state is Alaska. The largest state is Alaska.
38	Thanksgiving is in November. Thanksgiving is in November. Thanksgiving is in November.

39	Citizens elect the President. Citizens elect the President. Citizens elect the President.
40	We the citizens elect Congress. We the citizens elect Congress. We the citizens elect Congress.
41	The White House is here. The White House is here. The White House is here.
42	American Indians in Alaska vote. American Indians in Alaska vote. American Indians in Alaska vote.
43	The second President was Adams. The second President was Adams. The second President was Adams.
44	The right to vote is one right. The right to vote is one right. The right to vote is one right.

45	Citizens want freedom of speech. Citizens want freedom of speech. Citizens want freedom of speech.
46	The President meets the people. The President meets the people. The President meets the people.
47	The White House is in the capital. The White House is in the capital. The White House is in the capital.
48	United States citizens pay taxes. United States citizens pay taxes. United States citizens pay taxes.
49	Is Washington, D.C. in Washington? No. Is Washington, D.C. in Washington? No. Is Washington, D.C. in Washington? No.
50	Congress meets in Washington, D.C. Congress meets in Washington, D.C. Congress meets in Washington, D.C.

51	California has the most people. California has the most people. California has the most people.
52	Presidents' day is in February. Presidents' day is in February. Presidents' day is in February.
53	Washington is on the dollar bill. Washington is on the dollar bill. Washington is on the dollar bill.
54	United States citizens can vote. United States citizens can vote. United States citizens can vote.
55	Lincoln lived in the White House. Lincoln lived in the White House. Lincoln lived in the White House.
56	The flag is red, white and blue. The flag is red, white and blue. The flag is red, white and blue.

57	American Indians lived in Alaska. American Indians lived in Alaska. American Indians lived in Alaska.
58	Freedom of speech is one Right. Freedom of speech is one Right. Freedom of speech is one Right.
59	California is south of Washington. California is south of Washington. California is south of Washington.
60	The President lives in Washington, D.C. The President lives in Washington, D.C. The President lives in Washington, D.C.
61	New York City has the most people. New York City has the most people. New York City has the most people.
62	Adams was the second President. Adams was the second President. Adams was the second President.

63	One Right is freedom of speech. One Right is freedom of speech. One Right is freedom of speech.
64	Freedom of speech is one Right. Freedom of speech is one Right. Freedom of speech is one Right.
65	Washington was the first President. Washington was the first President. Washington was the first President.
66	The first President was Washington. The first President was Washington. The first President was Washington.
67	The people lived in Washington. The people lived in Washington. The people lived in Washington.
68	People come during Thanksgiving. People come during Thanksgiving. People come during Thanksgiving.

69	We can come to the White House. We can come to the White House. We can come to the White House.
70	Canada is north of the United States. Canada is north of the United States. Canada is north of the United States.
71	Mexico is south of the United States. Mexico is south of the United States. Mexico is south of the United States.
72	Delaware is south of New York City. Delaware is south of New York City. Delaware is south of New York City.
73	New York City is in the United States. New York City is in the United States. New York City is in the United States.
74	Come during Independence Day. Come during Independence Day. Come during Independence Day.

75	Most people have one dollar bill. Most people have one dollar bill. Most people have one dollar bill.
76	New York City is the largest one. New York City is the largest one. New York City is the largest one.
77	New York City is north of Delaware. New York City is north of Delaware. New York City is north of Delaware.
78	The White House is in Washington, D.C. The White House is in Washington, D.C. The White House is in Washington, D.C.
79	The United States has fifty (50) states. The United States has fifty (50) states. The United States has fifty (50) states.
80	The President lives in the White House. The President lives in the White House. The President lives in the White House.

81	Washington is the Father of Our Country. Washington is the Father of Our Country. Washington is the Father of Our Country.
82	People come here for freedom of speech. People come here for freedom of speech. People come here for freedom of speech.
83	Congress has one hundred (100) Senators. Congress has one hundred (100) Senators. Congress has one hundred (100) Senators.
84	The White House has the largest flag. The White House has the largest flag. The White House has the largest flag.
85	We have the Right of freedom of speech. We have the Right of freedom of speech. We have the Right of freedom of speech.
86	The Father of Our Country is Washington. The Father of Our Country is Washington. The Father of Our Country is Washington.

87	Lincoln was President during the Civil War. Lincoln was President during the Civil War. Lincoln was President during the Civil War.
88	Alaska is the largest of the 50 (fifty) states. Alaska is the largest of the 50 (fifty) states. Alaska is the largest of the 50 (fifty) states.
89	People come to the United States to be free. People come to the United States to be free. People come to the United States to be free.
90	People want American Indians to vote. People want American Indians to vote. People want American Indians to vote.
91	The President meets people at the White House. The President meets people at the White House. The President meets people at the White House.
92	Citizens elect the President and the Senators. Citizens elect the President and the Senators. Citizens elect the President and the Senators.

93	The President and the Senators pay taxes. The President and the Senators pay taxes. The President and the Senators pay taxes.
94	During the Civil War the President was Lincoln. During the Civil War the President was Lincoln. During the Civil War the President was Lincoln.
95	American Indians lived first in the United States. American Indians lived first in the United States. American Indians lived first in the United States.
96	The capital of the United States is Washington, D.C. The capital of the United States is Washington, D.C. The capital of the United States is Washington, D.C.
97	American Indians lived in the United States first. American Indians lived in the United States first. American Indians lived in the United States first.

98	One President lived in Washington D.C. and New York City. One President lived in Washington D.C. and New York City. One President lived in Washington D.C. and New York City.
99	Presidents' Day and Memorial Day come before Thanksgiving. Presidents' Day and Memorial Day come before Thanksgiving. Presidents' Day and Memorial Day come before Thanksgiving.
100	The one hundred (100) Senators vote in Washington, D.C. The one hundred (100) Senators vote in Washington, D.C. The one hundred (100) Senators vote in Washington, D.C.

<table>
<tr><td><h1>Finding Information Online</h1></td><td><h1>7</h1></td></tr>
</table>

HELPFUL WEB ADDRESSES

The names of the 2 United States Senators from your State: www.senate.gov

The name of your state's Governor: www.usa.gov/states-and-territories

The name of your Representative and the name of the Speaker of the House of Representatives: www.house.gov

To visit the Immigration and Naturalization Services' web page, including information on the Naturalization (Citizenship) Test: www.uscis.gov

FREE 16-minute USCIS video: You can see the official FREE 16-minute USCIS video which has an example of the interview by going to: https://www.uscis.gov/citizenship/learners/study-test (In the "Additional Resources" section at the bottom of the page, click on "USCIS Naturalization Interview and Test Video".)

<u>The Spanish version of this book</u>

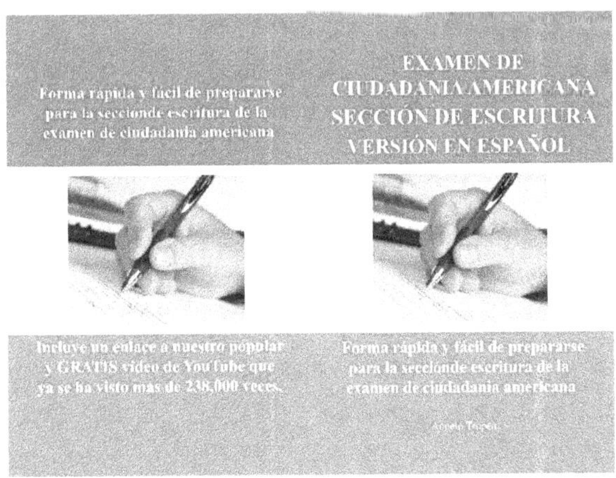

Another Book You May Like

EASY TO USE AND GREAT STUDY GUIDE FOR THE NATURALIZATION TEST!

COVERS ALL 100 USCIS OFFICIAL QUESTIONS AND ANSWERS - and all 100 Civics Lessons with EASY ANSWERS!

Everything you need for the reading and writing sections, including all the vocabulary and easy-practice sentences. Everything you need to pass the exam!

Includes:

1. Description of Naturalization Interview with USCIS Officer

2. All 100 OFFICIAL Civics Questions and Answers provided by the USCIS (U.S. Citizenship and Immigration Services)

3. All 100 OFFICIAL USCIS detailed Civics Lessons

4. All OFFICIAL reading and writing vocabulary

5. Complete list of sentences for reading and writing practice

6. Names of all U.S. Senators, U.S. Representatives, State Governors, and State Capitals

7. Links for other helpful websites